CONTENTS

DEALING WITH IDIOTS

A SHORT GUIDE TO NAVIGATING THE OFFICE JUNGLE

Upgraded Books

INTRODUCTION

It's really annoying walking into the office knowing that you'll need to deal with the same old idiots day in and day out. I mean, who doesn't get sick and tired of putting up with our beloved colleagues and their personalities all the time? It would be so much easier if we could navigate the office jungle without having to deal with their stupidity and just get on with our things, right?

In that spirit, this book will offer you a light-hearted, tongue-in-cheek guide to help you deal with all the annoying people in your workplace and your life generally. They're unavoidable, unfortunately. They're a fact of everyday life. But we can learn how to deal with them effectively.

You'll be like an office bird watcher, identifying different species by key personality traits. From the stubbornly resistant to change to the creatively chaotic, you'll find a varied assortment of character traits to work with.

We'll first encounter "Mark" in the book. This type is stubborn as a mule, resistant to any hint of change, and always insisting on doing things their way.

Next, we'll bump into Josh — the disorganized colleague who always seems to be living in their own world—the office whirlwind who keeps everyone on their toes with their last-minute habits and untidy workspace.

We've also got Suzanne — the misguided extrovert who's pretty much up in everyone's business and loves to be the center of attention.

You'll learn how to deal with each personality type and navigate the office jungle like a pro!

So, let's go ahead and make your office life a little less stressful and a lot more fun!

CLOSED TO CHANGE

If you've been in the workforce long enough, then you've met Mark. We all know Mark. We might even have a Mark in our family! Mark is the control freak who never ever wants to try anything new. You and your friends want to try that new Lebanese restaurant that just opened, but Mark would prefer to eat tacos *again*. You want to try a new location for vacation this year, but Mark thinks Cleveland is fine. Why fix it if it isn't broken? Besides, think about the costs, the stress, the planning, and the *uncertainty* of going somewhere new for your vacation. Is it really worth it? Is it? According to Mark, no, never!

You love Mark, but you have secretly calculated how much you spend on painkillers when you hang out with him. You've considered sending him an invoice for your painkillers, but since he's so stubborn, he won't pay it anyway! To console yourself, you tell yourself that at least you don't work with Mark. It's not much, but it comforts you. Imagine the poor sod who has to work with him on a group project!

At least you won't have HR breathing down your neck like an over-caffeinated jackrabbit when you inevitably tell Mark to remove the stick from where the sun don't shine and live a little. God knows you don't need a sexual harassment complaint on your company file in this economy.

Besides, Mark has a temper. Ironically, he often gets upset when his family refuses to support his chronic hard assness. His refusal to try new things stems from chronic anxiety: when people around him do not acquiesce to his demands for stability, he lashes out, an unhealthy coping mechanism that doesn't really help him in the long run. In fact, it has caused a few rifts in his friendships. When these rifts occur, Mark then finds an outlet for his anxiety by going to work determined to exert his full control over everyone. This is how Mark got the reputation for having a temper. That was the time he had a shouting match with the CFO about cutting Christmas bonuses and managed to get everyone's bonus back!

Although Mark might consider himself an angry person, this is all a cover for how he truly feels deep inside. A military general on the outside, deep down inside, Mark feels vulnerable in a world where he can never have full control. So, since control is what he craves the most in life, he tries to control others. Unfortunately, the unpleasant thing about control is that you sometimes use techniques that can be abusive to achieve it. Additionally, since he is used to people cowering from his anger and giving him what he wants, Mark never feels the need to self-reflect or work on self-improvement. As a result, he never picks up better techniques for getting what he wants that don't involve potentially harming others and taking away their power in the same way that his own bullies took away his power. Why become a more pleasant person to be around if being a hard ass works just fine? This approach misses the fundamental truths about personal and professional relationships - that they thrive on respect, understanding, and mutual support. Being genuinely likable and respected requires discipline, self-awareness, and emotional regulation - qualities that necessitate a willingness to be vulnerable and to grow, traits Mark's upbringing did not foster. Hence, Mark would rather inconvenience everyone in the office by installing an unapproved lock on the office kitchen fridge than simply sending a nice office email asking the office lunch thief (whoever they are) to stop eating his lunch. In response, HR, wary of confronting Mark directly due to his intimidating demeanor, opts for a workaround that, while seemingly practical, inadvertently reinforces Mark's controlling behavior: request the key from Mark whenever you need to grab your lunch.

It's been months of Mark (and the office lunch thief) terrorizing the office. You've made a decision that Mark needs to be stopped! But how?

NAVIGATING MARK'S MAZE

You've thought about acting just as crazy as he does. After all, people always say that you must out-crazy crazy, right? The only problem is you don't have it in you to match Mark's level of crazy. You don't have the hair-trigger temper, the terrifying glint in your eye when people question you, or the 80's cocaine kingpin energy to stand your ground when others challenge you. Mark seems to derive energy from starting WWIII with others, whereas the thought of bringing your tool set into work to install a lock on the fridge drains you of all power. Energy-wise, you are both mismatched. Plus, you seem to have a fear of consequences, a hindrance that does not seem to concern Mark at all. You have to hand it to Mark; he is a formidable force or, to put it more professionally... he has some big balls!

Since you can't out-crazy Mark, there is one more option available to you: you'll have to out-logic him. To defeat your enemy, you must first know your enemy. What are Mark's weaknesses? You already know his strengths. Whether it be his crazy energy, his refusal ever to back down, or his temper, Mark certainly makes a formidable warrior in battle. But every formidable warrior has their weakness. Just like every other person in the world, Mark's weakness can be gleaned from his childhood.

As a child, Mark grew up with a workaholic father who was never at home. Sure, he never lacked material things, and his family never worried about money, but Mark was often bullied at school because he was physically smaller than the other boys. When the bullying first began, his mother told him to ignore it. *"Bullies just want your attention. If you ignore them, they will go away."* Mark still remembered the advice she repeated to him every day after school, not particularly because it was helpful, but because of the pain and deep sense of powerlessness he felt when she said it.

All he really wanted was for his parents to come to his school and make the bullying stop, but neither of them seemed particularly interested in doing this. His father was too busy at work to really show any interest in Mark's life, and his mother dismissed his pain even when she noticed him becoming more fearful and anxious at home — an obvious response to the escalating bullying at school.

Eventually, Mark would experience a growth spurt that caused the bullying to stop almost overnight, but the damage was already done. What he remembered most wasn't even the bullying. Rather, what stuck with him was how he cried himself to sleep every night because he could not believe his parents loved him so little. He was so unworthy of his mother and father's love that they refused to protect him from those who humiliated and hurt him every single day. For years after, no matter how much he tried to ignore it, the pain of his parent's betrayal refused to ease. What was essentially the bruise of a childhood occurrence - bullying - transformed into a deep, unhealed wound at the root of his psyche, affecting all areas of his personality. Mark's bullies had stripped him of his power, and his parents had refused to get that power back. This pivotal childhood experience would transform Mark from a happy-go-lucky boy into the office terror you know now.

Today, Mark is hyper-vigilant of people trying to take his power away. Although all humans have inherent worth, Mark believes he is unworthy because his parents made him feel worthless when he needed them most. Since the way our parents treat us in childhood (and even adulthood) goes on to affect the way we see ourselves and interact with the world, Mark is now in a state of constant terror, always fearful that others will figure out his deepest secret: that he is worthless. So, to hide what he believes to be his inherent worthlessness, he exerts control and power over others and the world around him. If he can control everything and everyone around him, no one can expose his worthlessness. For Mark, powerlessness is for losers, and control is for winners!

And herein lies a critical weapon for navigating Mark's complex defense mechanisms Mark. Mark's deepest secret is that he feels he has no control over his emotions. And, in a sense, he is right. He doesn't. His parents, rather than guiding him through the challenges of his youth and teaching him to confront adversity with resilience and empathy, left him to navigate his emotional turmoil alone. Mark's case is a manifestation of a common human reflex: projecting our pain onto others to alleviate our suffering. His childhood, marked by a lack of support in facing his bullies, left him with a profound sense of powerlessness. As an adult, he seeks to compensate for this by exerting control over his environment and the people around him, mistaking dominance for the stability and validation he craves. This isn't about judging Mark — after all, mastering emotional regulation is a lifelong journey, with missteps even for those who've been given the tools early on. Like our habit of eating a disturbing amount of snacks whenever we feel sad. In all honesty, Mark is doing what we have all done at one point or another: using others as an emotional punching bag to release emotional pain. Thanks to his upbringing, Mark needs to find consistent relief from his feelings of worthlessness. So, in search of a sense of peace in his inner world, he tries to exert outer control. To use this information to your advantage, all you need to do is give Mark the sense of control he craves. Why not give him what he so desperately sought from his parents but couldn't receive? If you give Mark the feeling of worth and power, you disarm him and, in the process, neutralize his desire for control.

You can do this by letting Mark think your ideas are his. Since he always wants to prove his authority and his self-worth, once you implant an idea in his head, he will move Heaven and Earth to turn *his* idea into reality. With this technique, you are killing two birds with one stone. You make him do all the work actualizing your idea, and you get brownie points with him by allowing him to feel the sense of power and control that he needs to find relief from the sense of worthlessness he feels on a daily basis. Remember that Mark needs to feel powerful. Once he feels empowered in your presence, he lowers his defense around you, making him less likely to turn his ire against you. Competing with Mark only pulls your attention and focus from more important matters in your career. Hence, to retain your power in your professional life, keep Mark distracted by feeding him with what he needs: the feeling that he is the King of the office and soon to be King of the World!

SET BOUNDARIES

This does not mean that you do not set boundaries with Mark. Mark himself is no stranger to setting boundaries. If he were, he wouldn't put the lock on the fridge as a way to assert his boundaries with the office lunch thief (whom many believe to be Sharon from accounting, but that's beside the point!). With closed-to-change characters like Mark, you can only thrive if you regularly assert your boundaries against their shenanigans.

There's no denying that Mark's childhood experience was very traumatic. You don't cry yourself to sleep every night as a child without experiencing some form of trauma from it. Without getting the support that he needed, Mark's trauma eventually morphed into post-traumatic stress disorder (PTSD), a sort of constant state of trauma. His unresolved trauma had essentially frozen a part of his psyche at the age when he first encountered his deepest fears and insecurities: his childhood years.

Interestingly, when the human brain goes through a traumatic event, it stores as much information about the experience as possible. Then, following the experience, to protect you, your brain remains hypervigilant for signs that your trauma is about to reoccur. This is counterproductive because, to stay in this state of hypervigilance, your brain causes you to relive your trauma unceasingly in order to protect you from a probable trauma that may never occur. In short, Mark is going through his childhood pain every day because his brain thinks forcing Mark to relive the pain incessantly is the best way to encourage him to avoid any triggers that are similar to his traumatic experience. He is always hypervigilant of others trying to bully him and take away his power. Of course, reliving your trauma constantly only causes you to feel the same pain over and over again, keeping you in a state of high emotionality. It's a weird brain defense mechanism that worked well when we needed to survive in immediate danger, like a hungry tiger in our path. However, this mechanism does not serve us well when we don't need to be constantly on guard for immediate threats to our safety. The human brain has not learned how to shut down this mechanism when not required.

Unfortunately for Mark, he regularly struggles with symptoms of PTSD, including emotional distress, negative self-thoughts, feelings of hopelessness, difficulty maintaining close relationships with others, feeling detached from those closest to him, and fear of reliving his trauma again, i.e., being bullied again, Mark leans heavily into his coping mechanism, control, to seek relief from his symptoms and triggers. Without the right guidance, love, and support from his parents at that key developmental milestone in his life, Mark developed this unhealthy coping mechanism, telling himself that he would never let any bad thing happen to him again. Of course, this is impossible to achieve in a world where we never truly have any control. For instance, we can't stop the train from running late because a goose decides to rest on the tracks and refuses to move. And we can't stop our neighbor, Gary, from playing his podcasts really loud because he thinks it makes him sound intellectual. Like the annoying train goose and the everlastingly irritating Gary, we just have to accept that there are some things we can't control in this life.

Unable to accept this, Mark finds himself in a constant state of pain and distress. To soothe his overwhelming PTSD symptoms, he oversteps others' boundaries to gain the illusion of control. But, since he is still fully aware of how little control humans truly have in this wild cosmos, Mark is forced to attempt to exert maximum control on his life - and the lives of those around him - to achieve the barest sense of security and the tiniest relief from his PTSD. Consequently, despite not being your boss or supervisor, Mark insists on micromanaging your work or rejecting new ideas outright. A typical workplace interaction with Mark may go something like this:

"I think we should try a new paper brand for the office printer. The one we currently use is really bad. I mean, like, really bad. It doesn't make sense because we can get much better quality paper brands for nearly the same price, give or take a $50 difference annually. I've done some research on this, and I have a list of paper brands we can try. There's a brand called -"

"We don't need new paper disrupting the flow in the office. We have a good vibe in the office. Why change it?" Mark responds with shocking intensity.

"It's just paper," your colleague naturally inserts, confused, but this only seemed to infuriate Mark more.

Explaining to Mark that the new paper is better quality and cheaper only falls on deaf ears. He isn't interested in rational facts. Indeed, Mark is well aware of the many grunts of frustration that come from his colleagues on a daily basis, all of whom are tired of the paper ripping at the slightest touch. It's not that he is not a part of reality. It's just that no amount of logic or explanation will convince Mark to at least give the new paper brand a trial. Why? Because you are making suggestions that are interpreted as wanting control in the office. Mark cannot allow this. Always keep in mind that Mark operates from a highly emotional state. What Mark is worried about is that a better paper brand might change the office dynamics. The sense of control he finds from the current office dynamic allows him to create an imaginary shell of being safe, and this quietens his PTSD symptoms temporarily. If he loses the control he feels he has on others in the office, the illusion is broken, his PTSD symptoms are triggered, and he is back to feeling like the powerless, vulnerable child he was when he cried himself to sleep every night. It certainly isn't rational to be so worried about changing paper brands, but a traumatized brain is not a rational brain.

Until Mark decides to seek healing from his childhood, he will always see threats, even where there is none. Additionally, humans tend to continue and even escalate behaviors they are allowed to get away with, so if you do not set boundaries with Mark at pivotal times, you are only permitting him to escalate his stubbornness and control. Instead, try setting boundaries respectfully by assertively communicating your needs and limitations. If Mark insists on micromanaging your work or rejecting your ideas outright, you might say, "Mark, you know I value your expertise, and I need some creative freedom to perform my best on this project."

This is usually enough to enforce your boundaries at that moment. As a general rule, Mark will often try to cross your boundaries. You may need to occasionally reassert them when necessary. Although there will be times when it gets tiring, it helps if you change the way you look at it. Rather than seeing it as a tiring endeavor, see it as good practice for learning how to enforce your boundaries with strong personalities. There are a lot of Marks out there, so your boundary game must be strong if you are going to interact with them on a regular basis!

On the other hand, if Mark continues to overstep his boundaries consistently, don't feel as though you need to put up with it. Suppose you find yourself constantly overridden or shut down by Mark to a point where it is now beginning to affect your work and career prospects. In that case, you must deal with the issue by asserting stronger, more permanent boundaries: boundaries that are more difficult to subsequently overstep. It is always best not to confront Mark directly in a professional setting because interactions like that may end up causing you to come across as the bad guy. If you, known for your composed and collaborative nature, were to suddenly confront Mark or engage in a heated dispute, it could negatively affect your office's reputation. The more professional and strategic your method of confronting Mark is, the less likely you are to come off as a bad person. For example, you can schedule a one-on-one meeting and come prepared with data to support your ideas, saying, "Here are five reasons why the office will be a more efficient workspace if we change our paper supplier. I've noticed we have different views on this particular strategy, so I've compiled some research that I think could help us find a middle ground. Can we discuss how we can integrate our ideas to benefit the project?"

By deliberately opening the discussion with the idea of collaboration and teamwork, Mark will be less likely to bulldoze his will on the office as he typically does because this would not project the image he wants. We know that the illusion of control is incredibly important to Mark's psyche and self-esteem. If he believes you to be in control or to have some level of power over him, this causes him to go into defense mode instinctively. Hence, it is in your best interest not to make him feel as if you are challenging his power and control. This does not necessarily mean that you give up your autonomy and self-control within your interaction with him, but it does mean you always make him feel as though he is heard and his contributions are valuable. In this instance, you "find a middle ground" with Mark, as opposed to simply stating that your idea to change paper supplier is much better (even if it probably is).

BOOST SELF-ESTEEM

If Mark sees you as a threat to his very precarious self-esteem, he will automatically go into attack mode to defend his inner vulnerable child. What you need to do, even when asserting your boundaries, is to give him a sense of control so that he does not feel as though you are a threat to him. It would help if you thought about your interactions with Mark using logical problem-solving skills. But, ironically, your approach when interacting with him must always be emotional. Why? Mark does not respond to logic or rationality because his brain is always in a highly emotional state. You have to meet him where he is.

If Mark argues during the meeting that, despite your fact-filled presentation, the paper still should stay the same, don't argue with him. Instead, commend him for having the office's best interest in mind. Praise his work ethic and business savvy. Compliments are always a great way to get people on your side. This does not mean that the compliments should sound forced. Your compliments must be at least somewhat based on reality. Otherwise, they have the opposite effect and cause people to distrust you. By using compliments genuinely in your interactions with people, you build a natural connection with them, and, more importantly, you cause them to feel good in your presence. This will also go a long way in your relationship with people generally if you're able to make them feel good about themselves in your presence.

If compliments are one of the few ways in which you can get Mark to stop breaking your back for a minute and give you some breathing space at work, then dish them out with as much gusto as you can. Think about it this way: what strategy will negatively affect you the most? The first is Mark constantly shutting down all your ideas, preventing your career advancement in the process, which does not help. Slowly, this builds up, and eventually, you begin to act curtly and rudely towards him and are soon fired because you become bitter. The second way is to compliment Mark often so that he soon grows to like you and actually fights for your ideas when you bring them up in meetings. In the latter, your compliments are a replacement for the love and acceptance Mark did not feel he received from his parents. They make him feel good and soothe his PTSD symptoms, so he protects you fiercely. With the former, Mark sees you as one of his former bullies and becomes determined to destroy you with the same vigor he wished he had to stand up to them back when he was a vulnerable child. I know which method I'd choose!

And I know what you're thinking. It's not my job to love Mark like a parent. That seems to be way above and beyond my job description. It sure is, but do you want to be right, or do you want to have a job that makes your life easier? Learning how to deal with other quirky human characters is not part of our job description, but we must learn how to if we are to survive in our communities. It has been how humans have survived throughout history.

When you compliment Mark, you're doing something that most people don't do in his life, which is allowing him to feel a sense of power without having to fight for it. Since he is so used to people challenging his exertions of power and authority, you can instantly disarm him by complimenting (i.e., validating) his choices without putting up a fight. Any defense mechanisms he has up are also instantly nullified once you compliment him. If you do indeed need to challenge him, layer it between plenty of compliments so that he'd be too focused on his positive self-image to feel combative. When you use these psychological techniques, you give Mark the feeling of love and worth that he needed as a child, one that he is indirectly seeking through his power trips.

After management sees what effect your strategy

has on Mark, they may decide to follow suit to reduce the damage that Mark does in the office. To counteract the negativity stemming from Mark's resistance to change, someone in the management team may decide to implement a "Monthly Innovation" strategy, where team members can present new ideas or projects in a spirit of collaboration. This not only boosts morale but also gradually shifts the team's mindset towards embracing change. And, if you find that management does not implement this, why not take it to them yourself, presenting its benefits and how it can help the team?

REFLECTIVE SUMMARY

It's human nature to be resistant to change. However, people who bring innovation and change are those who do not allow the resistant-to-change characters to limit their ideas. While there are many reasons why a person may be resistant to change, this attitude towards change is usually, at the core, driven by fear, be it for fear of losing social status, fear of being seen for who they are behind the mask; fear of losing access to resources; or any other number of fears.

Fear, one of the most powerful human emotions, can be linked to anger, and anger, when turned on a person, is incredibly destructive. This is not to say that Mark and other resistant-to-change people are bad people. Nonetheless, history has shown us that when humans are under the grip of fear and anger, this can sometimes be disastrous. It is always in your best interest to dampen Mark's fear using tried and true methods like compliments, emphasis on collaboration, and cajoling him to fight for your ideas. When these coping strategies are used strategically, they disarm Mark by providing him with the comforting feeling of control on which his self-esteem is built. These psychological strategies also eliminate you as a threat to Mark. Out of his sight and off his blacklist, you automatically free up your time, energy, and resources, all of which allow you to focus on your own growth and happiness.

Likewise, these strategies also give you more time and energy to reflect on the ways in which you may also be resistant to change. Perhaps you share a lot of Mark's professional resistance to change and do not even realize it. Perhaps you are very open-minded professionally but hold on to control too tightly in your personal life. Whichever way being resistant to change manifests in your life, it can be an indication for some internal searching to discover why. By combining your intellect with your emotional insight and seeking professional guidance when necessary, you, too, can begin to heal from your own traumas.

Life will always throw us curveballs. Our ability to adapt is the key to thriving and growing, whether personally or professionally.

THE LOW CONSCIENTIOUSNESS TYPE

You glance at the time on your computer once again. Quickly, your eyes race upward to check whether you've received any new emails in the past two seconds. You haven't. He promised you that he would send the files by 12:00 pm yesterday. It is now 4:30 pm today, and you haven't heard a word from him. The presentation is due tomorrow morning at 8:30 am, and you specifically informed him that you will need another extra day to put the final touches on the slides.

You're not sure what to do. You have sent five emails since yesterday, and none of them have received a response. You're not even angry. You're just frustrated and anxious. This presentation could determine whether you get a promotion next month. You even explained to Josh the importance of this presentation not just to you, not just to the company, but also to him. If the presentation goes off well, he will get plenty of recognition at work, recognition that could transform into his career advancement. Yet, here you are with no communication from him and no updates on when you can receive his end of the presentation. Even if he sends it now, you will be staying up all night completing a presentation that should have already been completed by now. You don't do too well if you get less than eight hours of sleep, meaning that you won't be at your best during the presentation tomorrow.

The more you glance at the clock, the more you feel the first vestiges of anger bubbling up inside of you. Is Josh being deliberately inconsiderate? Did he forget to do his part? Could it be a case of simply having no respect for you? Does he not care about the job? You have to wonder if the boss had asked him to send the presentation yesterday, wouldn't he have sent it even earlier, not wanting to lose his job? Maybe he just didn't care about keeping his job. Maybe he was secretly a multimillionaire and got this job just to have a reason to leave the house. Would Josh give you a few million dollars for free if that was the case? You refresh the page another five times, and still nothing. No email from Josh. Would he even send the presentation today at this point? Your anxiety levels are now elevated. Normally, you would have confronted him face-to-face by now. But he is working from home today. When he works from home, Josh's performance tends to suffer even more. You don't know what to do.

Back in his home office, Josh has one thousand tabs open. He has not checked his email since yesterday because he lost track of that email tab. He tried a few times to look for it and even closed a few tabs in the process, but that didn't really help. The more he closed tabs, the more tabs appeared out of nowhere, like magic!

Josh also completed the presentation this morning. He had it in his mind to send it to you and offer a sincere apology for the late send, but he got a bit distracted when he smelt his toast burning. He did a bit of cleaning in the kitchen to get rid of the burnt toast crumbs - and to give his eyes a break from staring at the screen - then the day just sort of went away from him. As he now sits at his home office desk, he can't shake the feeling that there's something really important he's supposed to do. But what is it?

Josh stretches, tired from working on the presentation overnight. He usually wouldn't work overnight, not even when the boss requests a project, but he likes you and really hopes that you will get this promotion, so he pulled an all-nighter for the first time in his life. It was brutal! As he sips his seventh cup of coffee in the past twenty-four hours, his email notification rings again. Josh sighs. He wasn't going to find his email tab at this rate. With a deep sigh, he closes the entire window and opens a fresh new one, ready to tackle the barrage of emails fighting for life in his inbox.

With a sinking heart, Josh realizes that he forgot to send the slides to you *eight hours ago*!

THE CREATIVE COLLEAGUE

The low conscientious coworker is kind of like the airhead of the office. It's not like they don't want to submit projects on time or they want to disregard their email for days — it's just that they are in their own world. These are the people who park their cars sticking far out into the road and do not even realize it.

Now, you can wonder why exactly they act like this. Is it a hormonal issue? Do they have brain connections that are different from yours? Are they just naturally impulsive and more likely to be excited and distracted by shiny objects? Did they have a childhood where their parents never prioritized being diligent and responsible, so they struggle with it now? Do they just find the daily tasks of life to be so boring that they cannot muster even the tiniest bit of energy to do what they need to do?

You can spend your entire life questioning why the

low conscientious worker acts like this, but this is a complete waste of energy — for some people, this personality is developed by nurture, while others are more naturally this way. You can also try having a conversation with this colleague about how their behavior affects you, and so on and so forth. But it's not like you don't already have enough things in life to deal with, all of which require as much energy as you can muster. The low conscientious worker has been like this for a long time, so don't hold out any expectation of change by appealing to their empathy. Their very own behavior affects *them*, and they've learned to accept it, so you better accept it, too!

Josh was the kid at school who always left his school bag in class when his mom picked him up after school. He was also the kid at school who would raise his hand to answer a question and then forget what the answer was — or forget that he even had his hand raised when the teacher called his name. He never had enough time during exams - if he actually showed up on time for the exam, that is - and you know that he was definitely late for his first job interview after college. He was not the college classmate that you relied on when you had group presentations, and he often turned up to family gatherings clutching a tragic bag of salad because it was the only thing he could grab at his local deli at the last minute.

And yet, somehow, the low conscientious worker

still skates by in life. Sometimes, Josh makes you believe that we are in a simulation. Perhaps he's just a character that's coded to always be there no matter what. It's almost like the Joshes of the world live in a sort of magical world where they never do things responsibly, but things still work out for them. You know very well that if you tried to live the way they did, your life may fall apart in about five hours. Maybe even in less time. The more time you spend trying to figure out if you're in a simulation, the more time you spend away from your own professional responsibilities. Your character is coded for responsibilities, achievements, and leg day. Focus on that. The only energy you should expend when thinking about the office Josh is how to use his strengths to your advantage and how to mitigate his weaknesses so that his actions do not affect your own professional career. In this chapter, we will discuss such strategies so that you're well prepared to deal with the low conscientious worker.

SPOTTING THE CREATIVES

The first thing you need to do when dealing with a low-conscientious worker is to determine if they truly are Josh. That is, how do you spot the signs that one of your colleagues is a low conscientious worker? Some of the signs of a low conscientious worker include lower self-awareness than what is generally considered typical, less diligence, less discipline, a predisposition to being disorganized, poor time management, poor impulse control, and an inability to follow through on a routine task.

The low-conscientious colleague usually does not have high-achieving goals. Sure, they are happy to just get by in life, and this usually works, but eventually, what happens is that they plateau at a certain level because they do not have the necessary skills to push themselves past a certain professional level. Since you prioritize fulfilling goals like making sure a presentation is of good quality, meeting deadlines, being organized, taking cautious professional risks when necessary, projecting a reliable personality, being dutiful and dependable, and hard-working, these skills give you an edge over the low conscientious worker when it comes to career advancement. But, since Josh is not particularly interested in these goals, it is safe to say that you and Josh are on different life paths.

There will be tell-tale signs that a person is a low conscientious worker. That's typically the advantage of the office Josh. They are often very easy to spot in the wild. One of the classic signs is that they are usually late, be it late to work or late on project deadlines. The low conscientious worker will usually have an untidy office workspace. They may show signs through their physical appearance, too. Like unironed clothes, an unshaven beard they forgot about for weeks, or a mustard stain on their shirt that you see for many days in a row. They most likely will have a reputation in the office for not being reliable and for missing deadlines often. You will find most people may be hesitant to work with them on important projects.

COMMUNICATION STRATEGIES

As you already saw with the scenario at the beginning of the chapter, communication is a big part of your relationship with Josh. In general, a low conscientious person will not be the best at communicating in a timely manner. Usually, they may have unconventional thought processes, which means that their minds are racing from one thought to another. This can place them at a disadvantage when it comes to communication. Hence, it is best to have a direct number where you can reach Josh. It is easy for Josh to get sidetracked and forget to read or respond to written communication. By calling him or speaking to him face-to-face, you may be able to get what you need from him directly while you have his attention. Even then, you will also need to diligently send him regular reminders to keep him focused on what you need him to do. You will essentially be using up diligence and discipline skills for two people. While this may seem like a lot of work on your part, it is nowhere as much work you'll have as leaving Josh to his own devices. Plus, think about it this way: by using your skills for two, you are pushing yourself to become better. You are fine-tuning your discipline and diligence skills, a practice that will come in handy in the next stage of your career and in life in general.

DEALING WITH THE CREATIVES

One of the major strengths of your low conscientious coworkers is that they can be quite creative. Because their brain is running at high speed and going through brain pathways that most brains don't go through, they do tend to see life with very creative perspectives. That means that they do tend to have a lot to bring to projects. They have a way of adding magic and wonder to a project because of their spontaneous creativity. So, while they may show up late to a meeting, it is best not to let it bother you too much. If you get too annoyed, you might find yourself snapping at them, disrupting their creative process and expending your own energy in the process. A better way to handle them is to bring a bit of organizational management to their chaos.

You have to realize that, in Josh's mind, structure is optional. He does not consider it to be imperative. In essence, you will need to find a middle ground when planning and executing projects with him. Why not simply tell Josh that the meeting begins thirty minutes earlier than scheduled? That way, when he shows up twenty-five minutes late, he is still five minutes early!

Your project management and collaboration with Josh will always need to have a twist. This means you will need to also develop and flex your creativity skills in order to find a middle ground to bring the best out of him. If you know Josh is going to send those slides late if you leave him to his devices, why not offer to work together in the office where you can reign in some of his spontaneity and still put his creativity to good use? Your goal here is to seek innovative solutions to Josh's out-of-the-box thinking. You are turning chaos into opportunity at every moment.

Let's take another scenario. Suppose one of your colleagues is mad at Josh because Josh messed up the folder containing all the arranged invoices for the month. You can ask Josh to think of a creative system for cataloging the invoices electronically. The low conscientious worker loves creative endeavors because they know they shine when there are no limitations placed on them, and they have a novel project to work on. You have also turned what would have been a loss of face into a moment for Josh to shine — something which he may very well crave. By doing so, you have made a friend and a connection in the workplace.

THE DOS AND DON'TS

The low conscientious worker is a bit more unpredictable in his regular behavior than the closed-to-change colleague, so you will need to be able to think on your feet to find creative solutions that meet whatever situation you are currently in. They will always surprise you, regardless of how well you think you know them. This is compounded further by things like personality traits, natural inherent qualities, and past experiences. For example, one low conscientious person may not be organized, but you can count on them to at least show up most times, while another may be unambitious but actually show moderate signs of being organized. There is no one-size-fits-all to the low conscientious personality, which makes them a much more challenging person to work with if you are not used to coming up with creative solutions to workplace issues.

With these dos and don'ts, you have a blueprint for

coming up with solutions that you can work with within the workplace.

Do

- Encourage their creativity.
- Allow for flexibility, including not criticizing them just because they think or do things outside the box. Focus on results.
- Set gentle guidelines that give them an idea of your expectations. With these guidelines, you can also determine if they are progressing according to the project's objectives (even if they may be getting there in their own way).

Don't

- Micromanage. Micromanaging gives the kiss of death to any passion, spontaneity, or creativity that Josh brings. For Josh, being micromanaged feels like being forced into rigid structures. This is one of the worst feelings in the world for the low conscientious worker, and they will immediately shut down. So, instead of getting the project rolling and goals achieved (albeit in unconventional ways), the project reaches a complete dead end with no creativity involved.
- Stifle their spontaneity or creativity.

- Expect traditional organization. If Josh remembers things by writing them down on a napkin or his hand, then so be it. What's important is that he remembers, not that he writes things down on a legal notepad or on his laptop as is more typical.

THE BALANCING ACT

As much as you don't want to stifle Josh's creative and innovative process, you still need some type of organization and order, especially when you are working in a group setting. You also need to take into consideration that although you may see Josh's approach to work as creative, albeit non-traditional, others may have a more rigid and traditional view of work. For people like these, Josh will be interpreted as a chaotic worker and a threat to their productivity. When leading a team, you will need to maintain a balanced environment that is free enough not to stifle Josh's unconventional processes but still maintains order enough to leave everyone else feeling like their professional needs are also being met. Plus, as we discussed earlier, Josh thrives and produces results when his free-spiritedness is balanced with a bit of order. So, how do you maintain this delicate balance?

The first thing you must do is change your perspective on the issue. Diversity can and will work to your team's benefit. Your goal should be to bring the best out of the conventional and unconventional ways of working, merging them together to create an adaptable system that serves everyone. This system of integration will operate differently depending on the unique personality and characteristics of the people on your team. The best way to determine what serves everyone is to encourage a system of openness. Encourage everyone on your team to feel free to speak to you openly about their concerns. Let them tell you what works for them and what doesn't. Regular meetings where everyone can openly and respectfully discuss their needs without fear of repercussions are a must. The goal of these meetings is to allow everyone to come to a general consensus through compromise without the need to feel stifled or unheard.

In addition to open communication, balancing chaos and order should also be reflected in the workspace. Don't underestimate the impact of the office environment on your colleagues. Naturally, the low conscientious worker thrives in a space where he feels free. His office may resemble a mess, packed with what looks like toys, games, and an assortment of colorful items, but these are what motivate Josh to do his best. On the other hand, some people like a complete separation of work and play and prefer to have a more conventional, orderly, neat workspace. These two types of workspaces are quite different from each other, and one may find the other space offensive to one's visual sensibilities. In such cases, management may attempt to achieve diversity within the workspace by allocating rooms in the workspace that are designed to meet different needs and personalities. If Josh works better when he plays some Playstation during his lunch break, then why not allocate a room for entertainment? What you will find is that some colleagues who have operated with a more traditional work order might also enjoy this new way of eating lunch and decide to join Josh in the entertainment. At the same time, you can provide a quiet space for people who want time to decompress or just to focus on work in absolute silence. Even the low conscientious worker will benefit from this from time to time since their mind is always racing. A chance to slow down their racing thoughts will also empower them to remember deadlines, note creative ideas, finish pending projects, and bring some much-needed predictability into their unpredictable work persona.

REFLECTIVE SUMMARY

The Low Conscientious colleague is best described as a whirlwind. A whirlwind is wild and slightly unpredictable, and it creates a heavy mess in its path. At the same time, a whirlwind is powerful. It changes entire landscapes despite being present for a very short amount of time. It has a force that either sends others running to hide or, ironically, attracts others to chase after it. No two whirlwinds are the same, especially when it comes to the contents of each whirlwind, but we know enough about whirlwinds to know that they are strong, awe-inspiring forces. And, since they can be so destructive, to mitigate some of their destruction, we study them extensively.

By studying a whirlwind, you, too, can learn to harness your own creativity. You can learn how to free yourself from structures that may be too rigid, to become more spontaneous, and to allow your creativity to flow. In short, you can learn how to be even more professionally rounded by adopting some of Josh's positive characteristics. The beauty of the low conscientious worker is that there is much to learn from their unpredictability. Many people, turned off by their wild unpredictability, often disengage from them as much as possible. This leaves plenty of knowledge untapped about the potential benefits their creative chaos can bring in building professional and business success. Chaos does not have to be a bad thing, especially when it has the correct outlet. It brings diversity to a world where humans are obsessed with organization and order. Most of the best thinkers were innovative thinkers whose outside-the-box way of doing things led them to create new paradigms. These new paradigms are what we then adopt into our everyday lives, bringing order to their creativity and using this balance of organizational chaos to make our lives better.

The Joshes of the world challenge us, and they can make our lives better. Learn to harness their wild creativity to bring the best of both worlds into your organization.

MISGUIDED EXTRAVERSION

Every Friday, without fail, Suzanne drags in an insane amount of baked treats, ready to spike everyone's blood sugar in the office. Her signature bright smile is always plastered on her face as she greets every colleague with smug satisfaction. Before she places her tray of baked goodies down, at least two or three of your colleagues have met her at the kitchen counter to discuss whatever treats she brought in today — and, of course, eat a few before they all disappear. If there was a competition for the *Most Loved Employee* at your workplace, Suzanne would win without contest.

As if trying to outdo herself, she has invited everyone at work to hers for dinner and drinks many times. The morning after her famous dinners, you watch your colleagues walk into the office, still smacking their lips from Suzanne's cooking, as phantom roast beef and salmon packets tease their greedy throats. Truthfully, you have been the greedy colleague yourself once or twice - or more! - because her food is just so damn good, and you always have a blast at her parties. In fact, Suzanne has become so important to the office that last year's office Christmas party was moved from the office to her house. Your manager broke company policy because everyone was looking forward to spending time with Suzanne. Unsurprisingly, it was a blast, too! And, with her homemade eggnog, delicious finger foods, and perky, vibrant, joyous laugh, Suzanne solidified her reputation as the most liked employee in the company.

It isn't just her food, though. Suzanne just has a way of making people love her. She talks to everyone, regardless of who they are. She always has a smile on her face and a listening ear for anyone who wants to vent. Whenever anyone at work needs help, Suzanne is their first port of call because she is always happy to help without complaining or making excuses. Suzanne is a people person through and through. Consequently, she thrives in the modern-day office environment. Irrespective of her cooking, her inner qualities, and personal characteristics are what have allowed her to worm her way into everyone's hearts. Even yours! There is just one problem: Suzanne sits right opposite you at work!

In previous workplaces, you had shared a desk with your colleagues. Hence, you assumed that sharing a desk with Suzanne would be the usual boring workplace experience. You like your privacy, so sharing a desk with someone else feels quite invasive to you. And, as much as you love Suzanne, you adore her in smaller doses. The problem is it's difficult to get smaller doses of someone sitting seven feet away from you eight hours a day. Let's take last week's incident as an example when you came into work a bit agitated. Like anyone else would, Suzanne kindly asked you if anything was wrong. Not wanting to blur the lines between your professional and personal life, you told her that everything was fine. You received a couple of phone calls in the morning and hurriedly went outside to answer them. On your way back, you noticed Suzanne staring at you, trying to get you to divulge what your calls were about. You simply offered her a smile, a casual "Don't worry, it's nothing," and returned back to work, hoping she would get the message. Unfortunately, you underestimated one thing: the Suzannes of the world love non-verbal communication because they always have the option to pretend they don't understand what it is you're trying to communicate. After lunch, a text comes in. Suzanne, seeing the way in which you desperately open the text, strategically cranes her neck to read your private messages as discreetly as possible. With tact, you cover your phone screen, but not quick enough. Opposite the desk from you, Suzanne sits back down with a satisfied smile. She has confirmed her suspicions.

The next day, before you head out to lunch,

Suzanne not-so-discreetly hands you a list that she had stayed up all night curating. "I lost about five hours of sleep, but I was more concerned about your health, darling," she bellows. "Anyway, here's the list. It's a list of the best homemade cures for hemorrhoids, honey. According to my neighborhood watch group on Facebook, number one will clear you right up in one to two weeks."

This is not the first time Suzanne has caused you grief in her effort to be "friendly" and "nice." There was the time she decided your singleness needed an immediate cure and began talking to the women in the office, asking them why they wouldn't date you. At first, you hoped to ignore Suzanne; being tactful and not too firm would work. But now, her actions have caused you to be labeled as the office loser who can't get dates, possibly because of the hemorrhoids. Suzanne has gone too far!

IDENTIFYING THE EXTRAVERTS

To understand Suzanne, you have to first recognize that she lives in a very special world. In Suzanne's world, she is special. She is consistently praised, admired, and rewarded for being an extroverted person. The first thing you must understand about Suzanne is that she meets little to no resistance from others when socializing with people. And, like anyone who has not often heard the word "no" too often, this can cause problems when they do.

As the name suggests, the misguided extrovert is extroverted. Now, there is nothing wrong with being extroverted. Extroverted people are often the life of the party, wanting to speak with everyone, having no trouble turning strangers into friends, and enjoying spending time with as many people as possible. Where the average extrovert differs from the misguided extrovert is that the latter has not learned how to mature their extroversion. This person is extroverted but assumes that being extroverted and having a natural ability to be socially gifted automatically equates to having emotional intelligence. As a result, the misguided extrovert may have no reservations about making conversation with people but will find themselves asking inappropriate, private questions at times — a trait of people with underdeveloped emotional intelligence. They may gain energy from spending time with and talking to people (a common trait of extroverted people) but remain unaware that this action leaves the other party feeling emotionally drained (this often happens to people who are introverted). Because they are outgoing, they ask you out for after-work drinks and assume you will naturally say yes, as that's what they would do if asked. If you say no, they react negatively and internalize your rejection of the offer as a rejection of their personhood. Why? Because people often do not reject the opportunity to hang out with them.

For the misguided extroverts, their extroversion has not yet developed properly, perhaps because they have not had many people challenge their behavior in the past. Look around you, and you will see that most people genuinely enjoy being in the company of extroverts, offering them plenty of positive reinforcement for their personality style. We live in a society that's ideally suited for extroverts, but this can lead to a sense of entitlement to other people's love, time, and attention when an extrovert is not fully developed emotionally. Sometimes, misguided extroversion is also borne out of childhood trauma.

Children who face neglect and abuse at home may put on the mask of extroversion in a misguided effort to "earn" the love they never received at home. Since this particular extroversion is borne out of unhealed pain, it can become counterproductive. Until this type of misguided extrovert is ready to face their pain and heal from it, they will continue to gloss over it, regardless of how many times their behavior may be challenged by others. The issue is not that this person is extroverted. The issue is that they are channeling their emotional traumas through extroversion. They know that people are apt to accept extroversion without challenging it. The deeper issue with the misguided extrovert is that, underneath it all, they need to heal.

This is why spotting a misguided extrovert can be challenging, especially when you don't know a person well. Misguided extroversion is often easily mixed up with just being extroverted. You will need to interact with a person a few times before you can begin to spot the signs. Suzanne may be able to make friends and create a community because of her extroversion, but if you watch your colleagues closely, you will realize that there are gaps in these connections. Suzanne's emotional immaturity leaves her only able to form bonds with people who share this same level of maturity as her. For those people who are more emotionally developed, they may keep Suzanne at arm's length, just as you do. While Suzanne might be popular, see if she has any close friends. Notice if they talk about anything apart from conversational things. Notice if she always seems to be joking around with people but hardly has difficult conversations or conversations filled with substance in them. Notice if she tells the truth gently and with love or if she just smiles at people and prefers to be friendly over telling the truth.

Like any other extrovert, Suzanne will very likely love to talk. Her gift of gab is exactly what earns her so much social capital in the workplace. She knows a lot, not only about her coworkers but upper management as well. She may often speak or act without first thinking. Everyone knows posting the problem of your colleague's hemorrhoids on your local Facebook group is not the action of someone who thought things through. God knows if she added personal information about you, it makes you identifiable in real life. And God knows if her post was shared many times. The point is, since the world operates with extroversion being the norm, an extroverted person can easily get away with emotional and social immaturity. That's the point! Their extroversion is often mistaken for emotional intelligence or mature social skills.

Sooner or later, you will encounter a misguided extrovert at work. They are sometimes known as the "personality hire," i.e., the person hired because they can easily charm people. With their charm and gift of gab, they are able to gain many friends in the office. They weave seamlessly through office politics, never really taking sides or being affected by any of it. This places them strategically in a social position where they naturally hold the power to promote office culture, bridge gaps in relationships, and unofficially be in charge of making the workplace happy. To spot the misguided extrovert in the office, you can look for clues that they may be a personality hire.

Another version of the misguided extrovert is the office mother. This type of misguided extrovert pays particular attention to how everyone feels. She cares for people in the office in a similar way to how mothers do and, by doing so, wins the love and admiration of everyone. After all, who doesn't love caring, attentive moms? Mothers, like personality hires, are also unofficially in charge of office culture. You will be able to spot the misguided extrovert mother because she uses manipulative tactics that emotionally unhealthy mothers may sometimes use on their children. For example, in response to hurting you, she may say things like: "I'm only doing this because I care about you. I didn't know you would get so mad," or any such variant. Phrases like these are meant to elicit guilt, implying that they sacrificed to make you happy, and you only paid them back by breaking their heart. It is meant to make you stop questioning their motives and accept that they harm you out of love. If you decide to hold her accountable despite this, she may then ask other people if she is such a bad person since, after all, she did it to help you. This tactic gets people in the office on her side, regardless of how much she actually hurt you.

To be clear, the misguided extrovert isn't a bad person. They are to be admired because they understand how social dynamics work. They understand how to make friends and influence people, a very strategic power that will take you far in life. The only problem is that they take their position in the social dynamics a bit too seriously, which can manifest in unhealthy ways to those around them.

DEALING WITH THE EXTRAVERTS

The misguided extrovert has usually been rewarded for their extroversion for so long that it has now become their only identity. Let's go back to Suzanne. She is a wonderful lady who has a natural ability to make people feel good about themselves. But on the flip side, like most humans, she guards her identity very seriously. If she feels as though you are challenging or criticizing who she is, she will go into defense mode. And, like most people who still have to grow emotionally, she interprets any action that is not instant acquiescence as a challenge or criticism against herself. People love and reward Suzanne's extroversion so much so that anything but the same high level of admiration from you will be interpreted by her as a deliberate ego wound towards her. And what do most humans do when they feel their ego is bruised? They try to take this power back by over-asserting themselves.

Some misguided extroverts might try to win over your admiration by ceaselessly being in your face.

Naturally, this will only cause you to push back from them even more, creating a never-ending cycle where you both feel frustrated, angry, and tired. Others may go the opposite direction and begin to dislike you from afar. To protect themselves from their feelings of rejection and low self-worth, they project these feelings onto you as anger. This leaves you at a disadvantage because emotionally underdeveloped people might do things like sabotage people who they perceive as not liking them.

Whether you're an extrovert, ambivert, or introvert does not matter. The Suzannes of the office can be challenging to work with sometimes – although they do tend to act with the most misguided energy around introverts. In the case of introverts, opposites repel rather than attract. For more introverted people, Suzanne's energy can be a bit much. An introverted person is more likely to turn down an invitation for after-work drinks, easily bruising the ego of an unsensing extrovert. Indeed, you might be a mature and developed extrovert yourself who finds Suzanne's refusal to respect your autonomy and boundaries just as challenging as an introvert would. Regardless of whether you are an introvert, ambivert, or extrovert, small misunderstandings, over time, can soon lead to bigger resentments and grievances between you and the misguided extrovert.

Before long, colleagues will pick up on this too. Since

Suzanne has her friendly image and warm, outgoing reputation on her side, people will be more apt to automatically see you as the antagonist in this situation. Everyone else in the office loves Suzanne, so you really don't want to be seen as her enemy. People will simply turn against you. Even if there are a handful of people who also find Suzanne's misguided extraversion to be a bit much sometimes, they don't want to be seen publicly taking that position, so they are not likely to back you if any tension arises between the two of you.

Like most extroverted people, Suzanne always finds herself the pillar of her community. That means that you won't always be able to avoid the misguided extroverts in your life. While misguided extroverts are well-known for their friendliness and niceness, they also wield a lot of power as the community pillar. Being friends with many people gives you social capital, and social capital can be power. Misguided extroverts are also usually aware of how much power being friendly gives them, so they may choose to use this power against you. In addition, humans are generally followers. This further boosts the power of a misguided extrovert who can easily sway people to their side. Hence, calling Suzanne out publicly will not serve you. HR will tend to side with the people in the office that they like despite what they may tell you about corporate policy — unless, of course, something truly egregious happens, which would be a significant liability to the company.

Conversely, you can always try speaking to Suzanne privately about her behavior. However, this can be a gamble, depending on her current mental state. You will need to judge the situation accordingly to determine if this is a risk you should take. Note that Suzanne may decide to share this conversation with strategic people in the office, choosing to share only select parts of the conversation that may not put you in the best of light and could potentially harm your reputation.

On the surface, it seems as though dealing with the misguided extrovert is a minefield, where every decision you take only leads to more complications, but this isn't necessarily true. As with all things in life, being a misguided extrovert comes with certain disadvantages. Sure, Suzanne is popular, has influence and power, and can impose her will on others with ease, but this also leaves her at a disadvantage. Since she relies on her social skills to move through life, chances are she has not fully developed her emotional intelligence. Think about it. If people like you immediately upon meeting you, then there is less incentive to study people and develop an understanding of what people think and feel and how to respond to them. People tend to give passes to those they like. And although this sounds like a good thing in theory, it can leave you at a disadvantage because people often won't call you out. Challenges are what improve us. But if people don't challenge you when you cross their boundaries or hurt them, then you can't develop your emotional intelligence. In short, you do not develop an understanding of how people truly feel about your words and actions. Likewise, you also do not know how to relate to people without the friendliness and charm of safe buffers. Consequently, you find yourself unable to handle communication with a more emotionally intelligent person. And this is the misguided extrovert's Achilles heel.

Now, you really do like Suzanne. But, at the same time, you are aware that your reputation is a very valuable form of social capital that must be protected. If you decide to apply for a higher role in the company, your reputation, alongside your experience and qualifications, will decide if you get the job or not. Even things like credit scores and legal records are a form of keeping information about a person's reputation and character. The more positive your credit score and legal record, the higher the level of opportunities and status you are given in life. Therefore, to protect your reputation from the misguided extrovert's misguidedness, you must use emotional intelligence to beat them at their own game of social popularity.

After Suzanne loudly informs the office that you have hemorrhoids, thank her loudly for her care and support so that the same people can hear you. Your response should go something like this:

Wow. How thoughtful! I know you didn't have to do this, Suzanne. Thanks so much! You're the best! I'm not sure if all of these will work for my sister's dog. She's tried everything to get rid of his hemorrhoids, but still nothing. But some of these ideas should work! I'll send this to her tonight! Thanks, love!"

You are well aware of how people might feel should you confront Suzanne for reading your personal text messages, as we've discussed earlier in this chapter, so it's best to avoid this. Instead, you beat her at her own game by also covertly crossing her boundaries. Sure, you might be fudging the truth. But on the other hand, Suzanne did invade your privacy and read your text, right? And Suzanne cannot exactly demand to reread your personal messages during office time to make sure she got it right — especially after calling people's attention to herself. By keeping yourself two steps ahead of Suzanne's thought process, you can neutralize whatever damage she may cause while still staying on her good side. You complimented her, thanked her, and accepted her gift with grace. She has no reason to dislike you and will simply have to believe that she read your text wrong. Is it gaslighting? Yes. But should Suzanne have not told the office about your hemorrhoids? Also yes. By taking this approach, you and Suzanne both get to keep your social capital intact without any animosity! You have also learned a very important lesson regarding your coworker: always read your messages away from the office or whenever she takes a sick day!

THE DOS AND DON'T

Do

- Use your emotional intelligence to think of creative ways to neutralize their misguidedness and keep your own reputation intact. The misguided extrovert is very aware of their social reputation. So you must always play that against them.

- Practice good responses to get you off the hook. It helps if you have some prepared responses so that you're not caught off guard when the misguided extrovert interacts with you. For example, it helps to have a few credible responses in case the misguided extrovert asks you out for after-work drinks. Saying something like, "I would love to, but I have a doctor's appointment at Gladesville I need to get to," or "I can't because I need to wash my eyebrows tonight," allows you to prioritize yourself and protect your privacy without offending

Suzanne.

Don't

- Make yourself too available to them. It can get tiring constantly thinking of emotionally intelligent ways to respond to Suzanne. So, a better strategy would be to avoid her as much as possible. For example, you could always go to HR and ask to be moved to the other side of the office. All you need to do is give them a believable excuse. You sit under the AC and find yourself catching a cold frequently, missing many work days as a result... Your religion does not permit you to sit under ACs, so you must move immediately... The lights are too bright in that area, and you're constantly getting migraines, which are affecting your work... Of course, you won't discuss this with Suzanne until the day of the move. This gives her less opportunity to be all up in your business. And, pending HR's approval, you've suddenly developed a taste for audiobooks and have to leave your headphones on all day. This means you can't chat with Suzanne like normal. Plus, even without the audiobook, you have deadlines and just can't find the time to chat with Suzanne. What a shame! And, even if you could, you stupidly ate garlic waffles for breakfast and can't chat today for fear of inconveniencing everyone in the office with your bad breath... the excuses available to you are innumerable!

- Neglect your relationship with others in the office. It is always a good idea to have a good relationship with your colleagues. Remember that the more alliances you have, the more social capital, power, and influence you also have. This way, you also gain the social leverage that Suzanne has, leaving you both on equal footing in the office. You don't necessarily have to copy Suzanne's style of making friends. You can always find what works for you and use that to build good relationships with others in the office. This way, you always have social guarantors who can also defend you in case Suzanne directs her misguidedness at you. For example, turning down after-work drinks with Suzanne becomes easier if you have another coworker chime in for you with a "She needs her rest! She's been working flat out on that project for months!" Without even saying a word, you get out of drinks you don't have the emotional energy for, keep your social capital intact, and manage not to offend Suzanne, either.

Don't make the mistake of directly communicating with the misguided extrovert about their behavior. Their misguidedness is just another word for emotional intelligence that is not yet fully developed. In general, a more emotionally intelligent person will lose more when trying to directly communicate with someone like that. Instead, use your own more evolved emotional intelligence to avoid directly confronting them while still indirectly putting them in their place, minimizing their damage to your social reputation, and maintaining good relations with them.

SUMMARY

Before diving into the book summary, I would be incredibly grateful if you could take just 30 seconds to leave me a review!

Reviews are crucial for an author's livelihood and surprisingly difficult to come by. The more reviews my books receive, the more I can continue pursuing my love for writing. If you have any thoughts about this book, please leave a review and let me know :)

Closed To Change

Mark is the kind of colleague that's resistant to change. He has a stubborn nature and control issues stemming from childhood experiences of bullying and a lack of parental support.

Mark operates from a highly emotional state due to unresolved trauma, making him hyper-vigilant about maintaining control.

Strategic Persuasion

- Recognize that Mark's traits stem from his

childhood experiences and his need for control.
- Suggest ideas in a way that makes Mark believe they are his own. This taps into his need for control and can get him to implement changes without resistance.

Provide a Sense of Control

- Give Mark a sense of control by validating his ideas and contributions. This can disarm his defensive behavior and reduce his need to exert control over others.

Set Boundaries

- Regularly assert your boundaries to prevent Mark from overstepping. Use respectful and clear communication to convey your needs and limitations.

Manage Emotional State

- Approach Mark from a place of calmness and patience, understanding that his reactions are driven by deep-seated emotional issues.
- Be mindful of potential triggers that could escalate his emotional state and avoid them when possible.

Low Conscientiousness

Josh is the typical disorganized and forgetful

colleague. Due to his lack of awareness and discipline, he often misses deadlines and is unreliable. He also gets easily distracted and forgets important tasks.

Face To Face

- Speak to Josh face-to-face or call him directly to ensure he understands his tasks.
- Send regular reminders through email, Slack, and so on to keep him focused and on top of deadlines.

Encourage Creativity

- Encourage Josh's spontaneous creativity to develop solutions, products, and so on. Allow for non-conventional methods for his work process while guiding him toward project goals.

Managing Chaos

- Provide a workable framework to help Josh stay organized without stifling his creativity.
- Offer to work together in the office to help him stay focused and meet deadlines.

Misguided Extraversion

Suzanne is the overly extroverted colleague. She is friendly and social and often crosses personal boundaries. However, she lacks emotional intelligence and becomes overly involved in others' businesses.

Set Boundaries

- Establish clear boundaries to protect your privacy and personal space.
- Use non-confrontational language to set boundaries.

Empathetic Approach

- Approach Suzanne with empathy. Try to understand her motivations and insecurities.

Conversational Toolkit

- Gently deflect any of Suzanne's intrusive questions and redirect the conversation to safer or more comfortable topics.
- Offer genuine compliments to Suzanne to keep interactions positive and reduce potential conflicts.
- Prepare ready-made responses for declining social invitations or avoiding intrusive conversations so that you're not caught off-guard. It can be as simple as "I appreciate the invite, but I'm focusing on some self-care tonight."

Made in the USA
Las Vegas, NV
31 July 2024

93171176R00046